SIMON JOHNSTON

MERIDIAN

PHOTOGRAPHS OF ENGLAND TAKEN ON THE LINE OF ZERO DEGREES LONGITUDE

00° 00′00″

01.

00° 00′ 00″ longitude: North Sea near Waxholme, East Riding of Yorkshire: △N

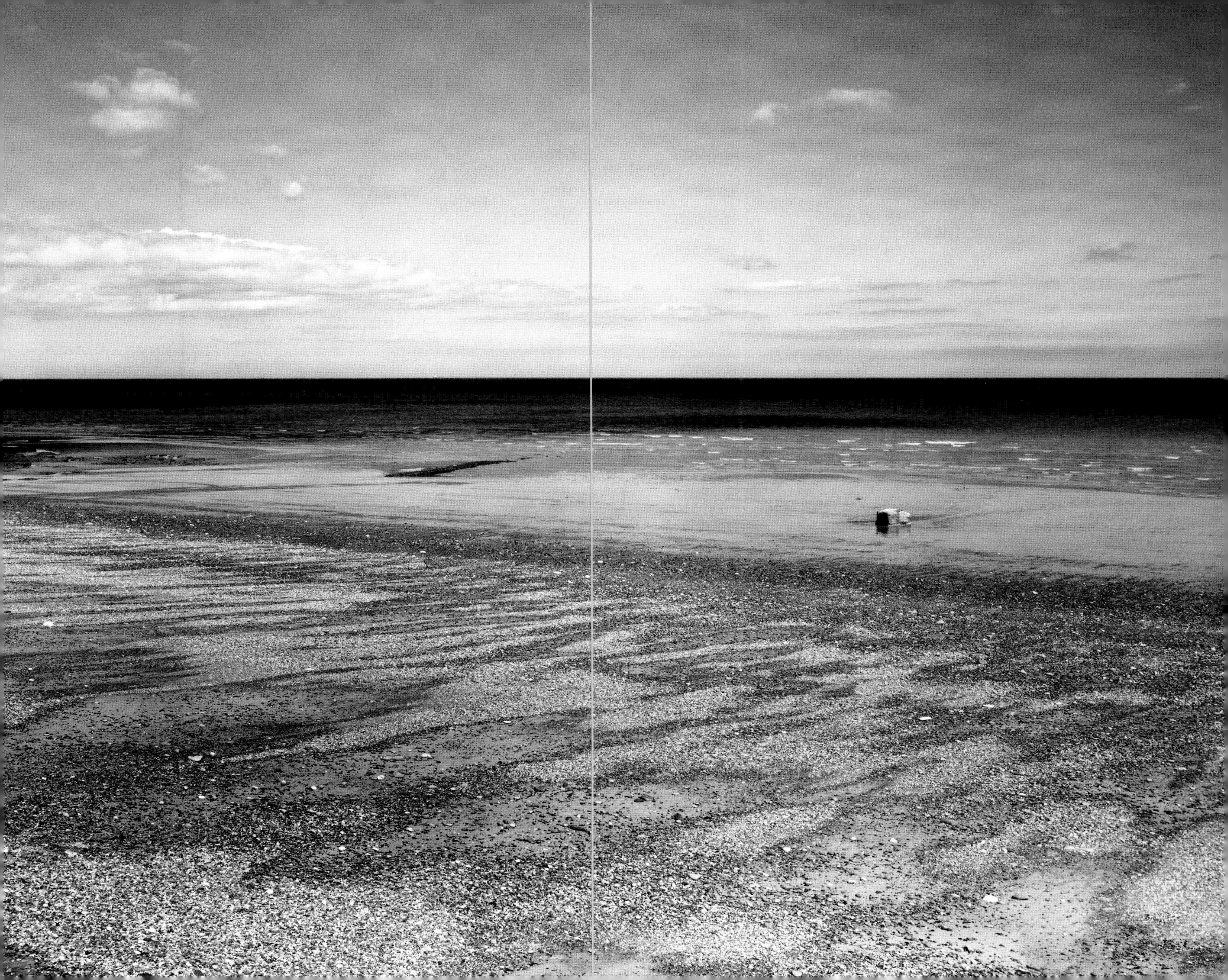

02.

00°00'00" longitude: Waxholme coast, East Riding of Yorkshire: ▽̄ S

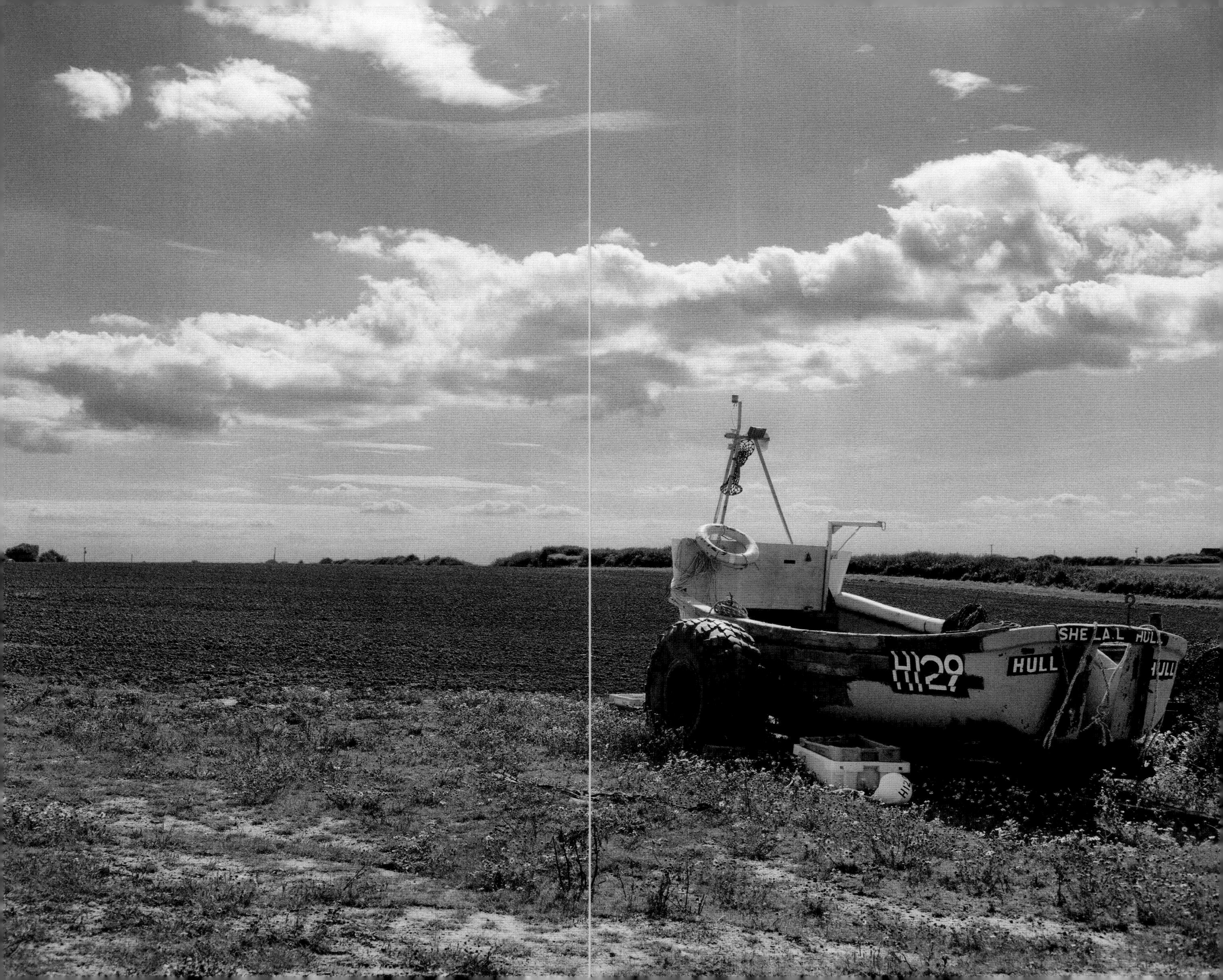

SHE LA L HULL
H129
HULL
HULL

03.

00°00′00″ longitude: Near Withernsea, East Riding of Yorkshire: ▽S

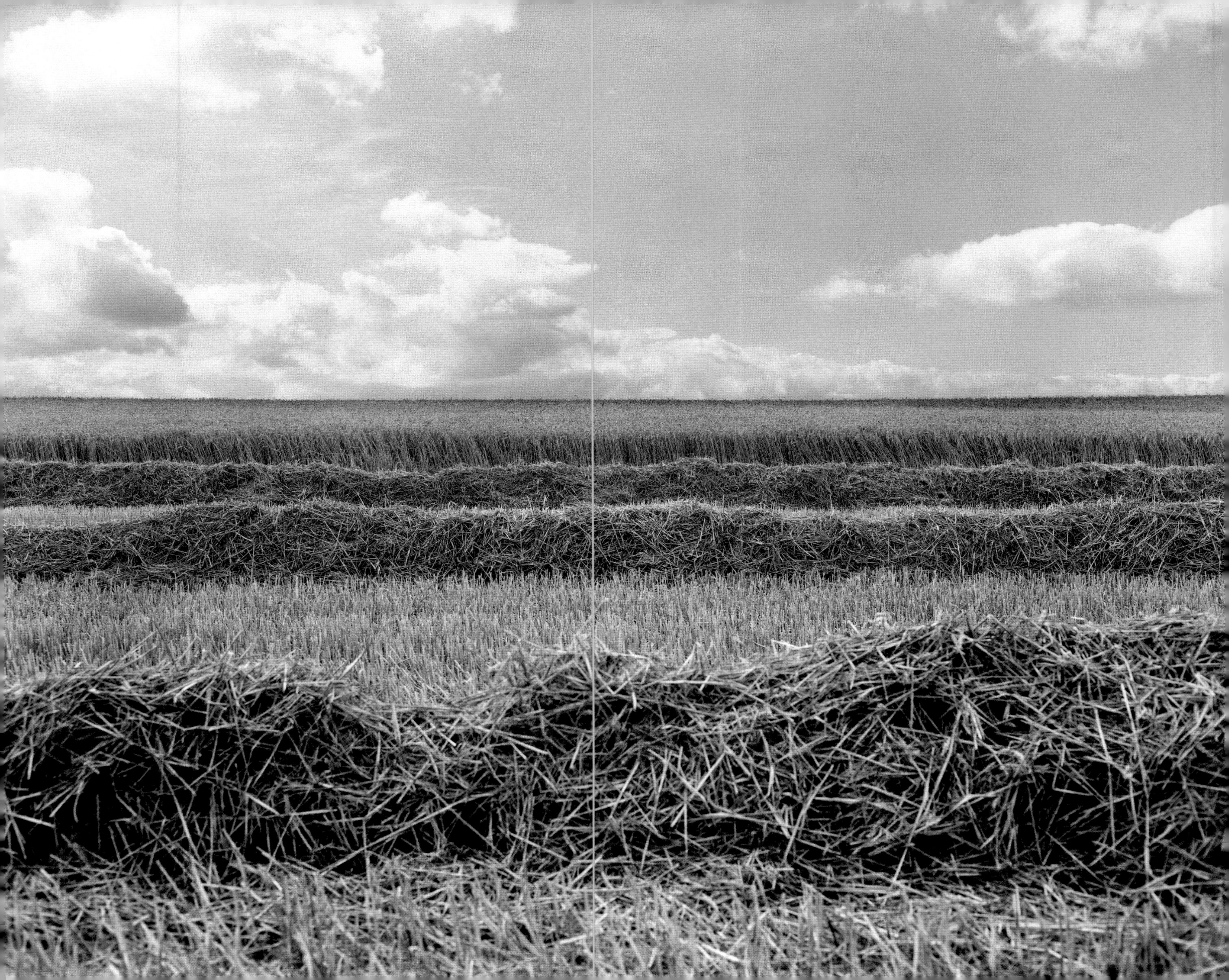

00°00'00" longitude: Humber estuary near Sunk Island, East Riding of Yorkshire: ⏝S

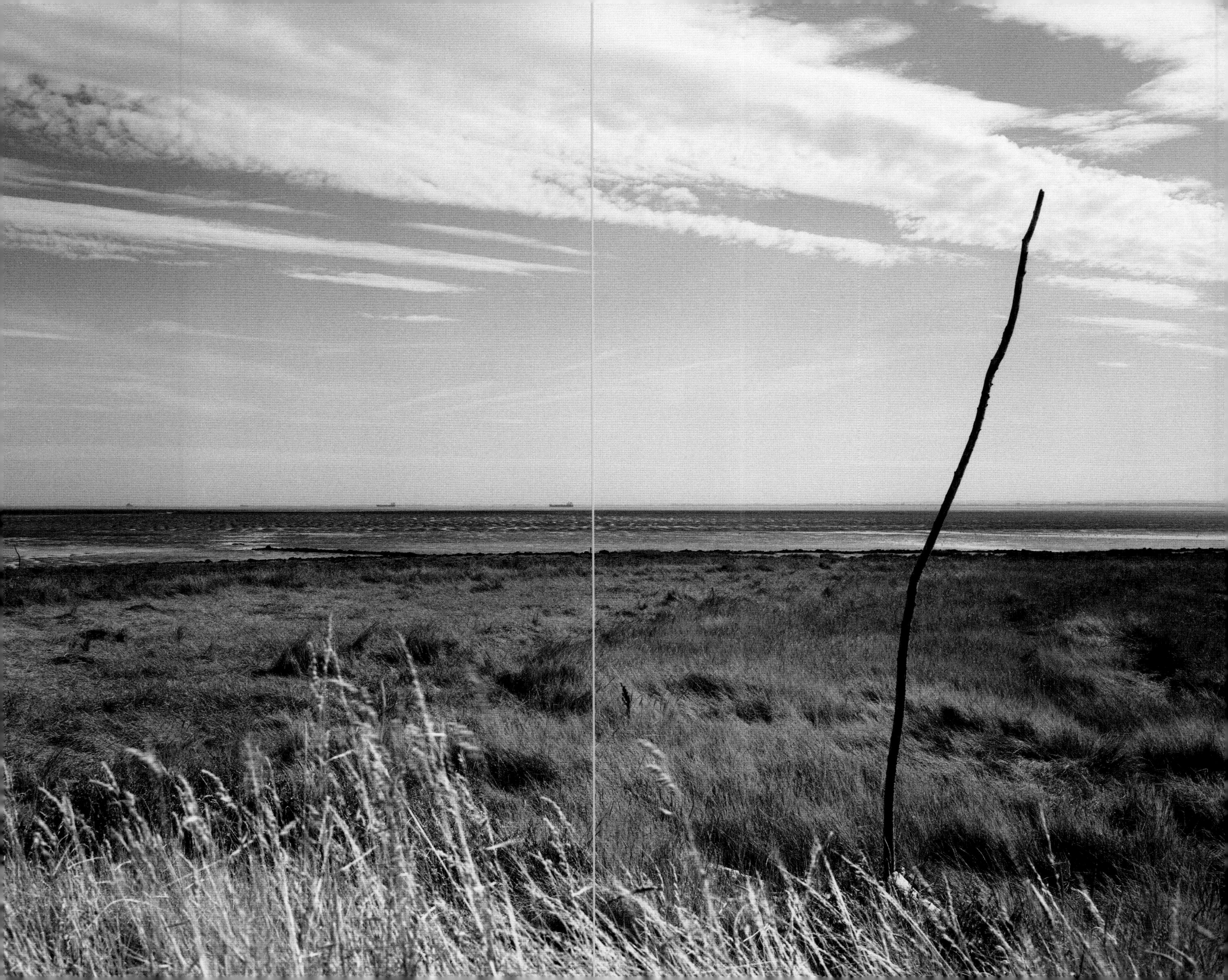

05.

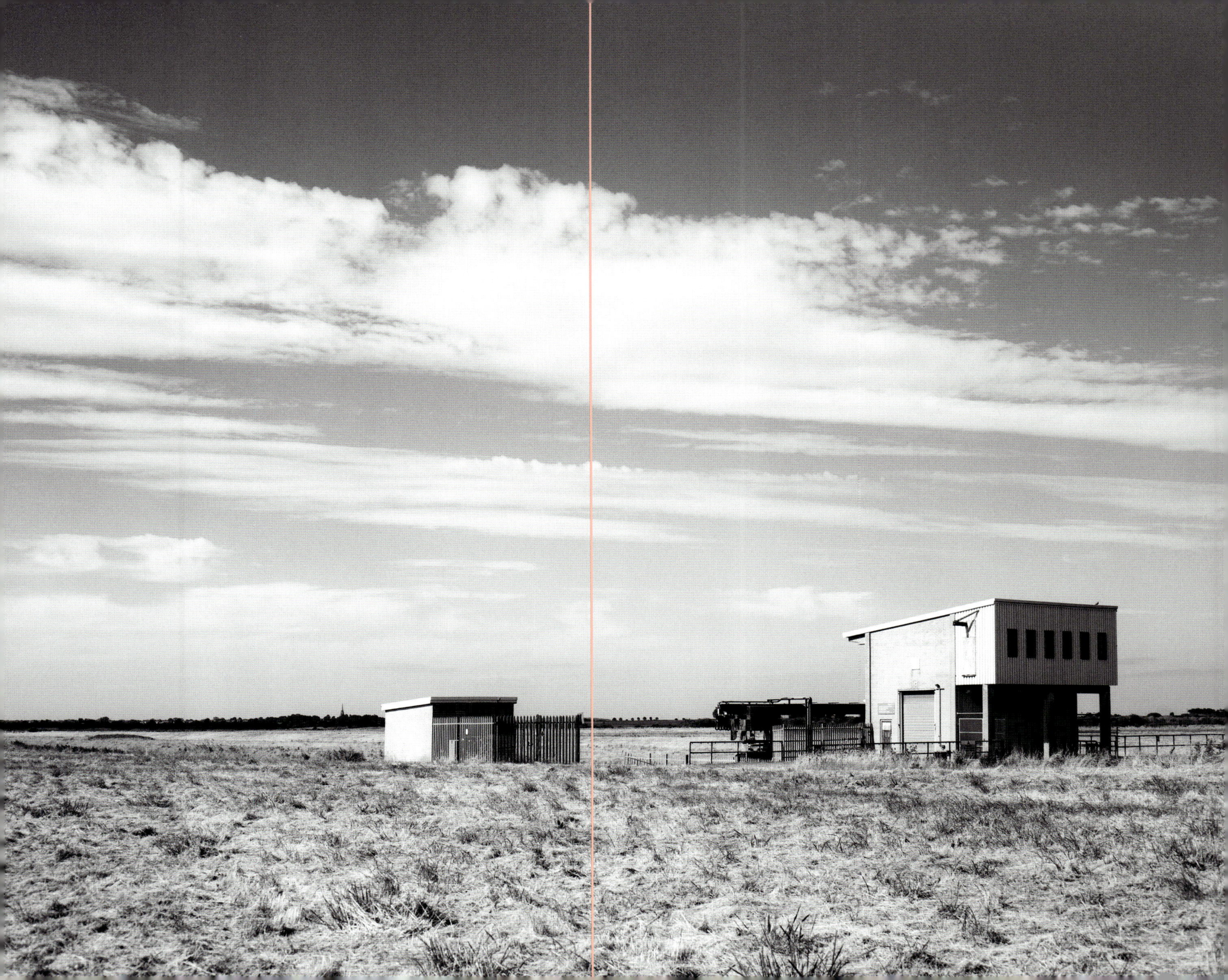

00°00′00″ longitude: Pleasure Island, Cleethorpes, Lincolnshire: △N

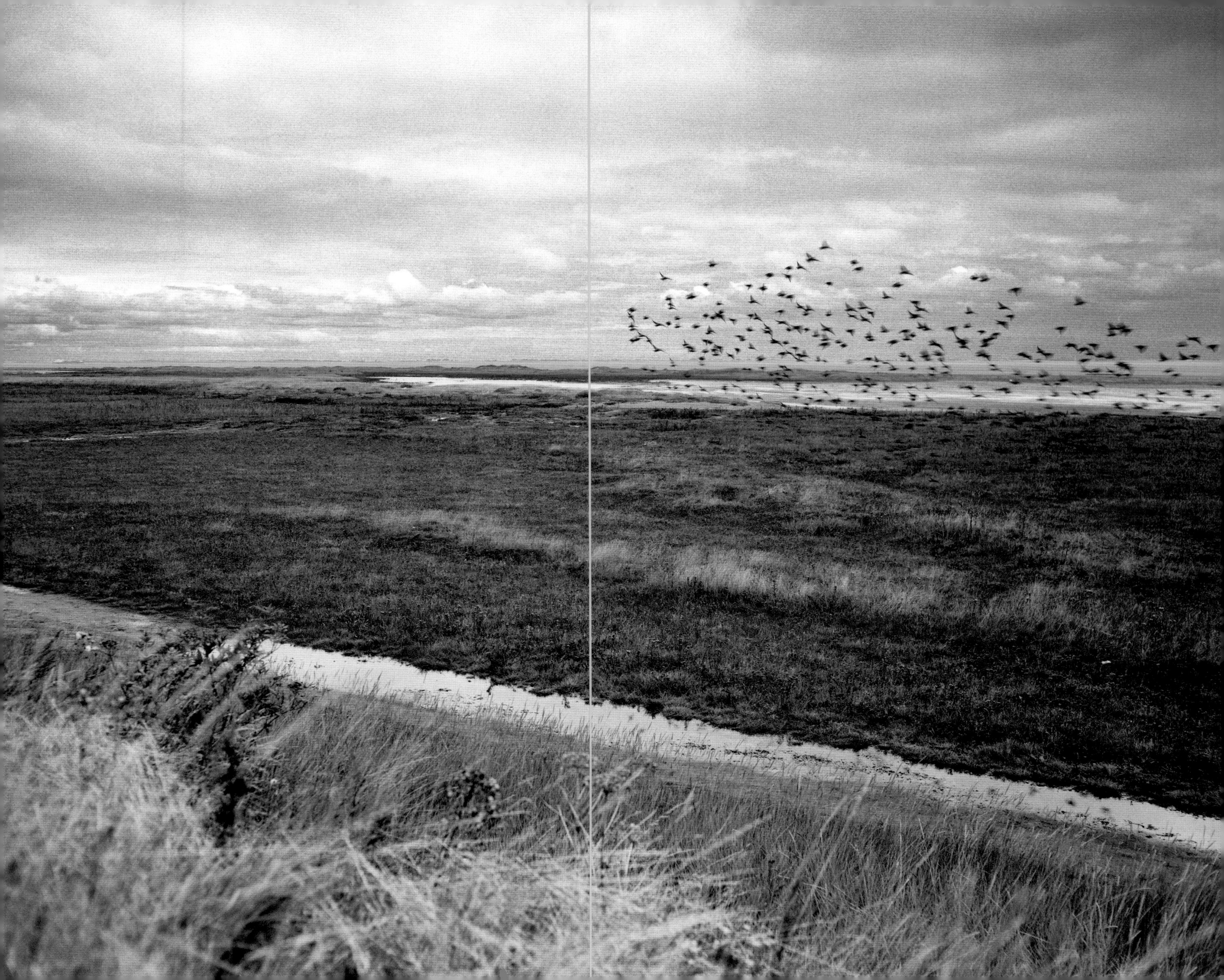

00°00'00" longitude: Near Harrington Hall, Spilsby, Lincolnshire: △N

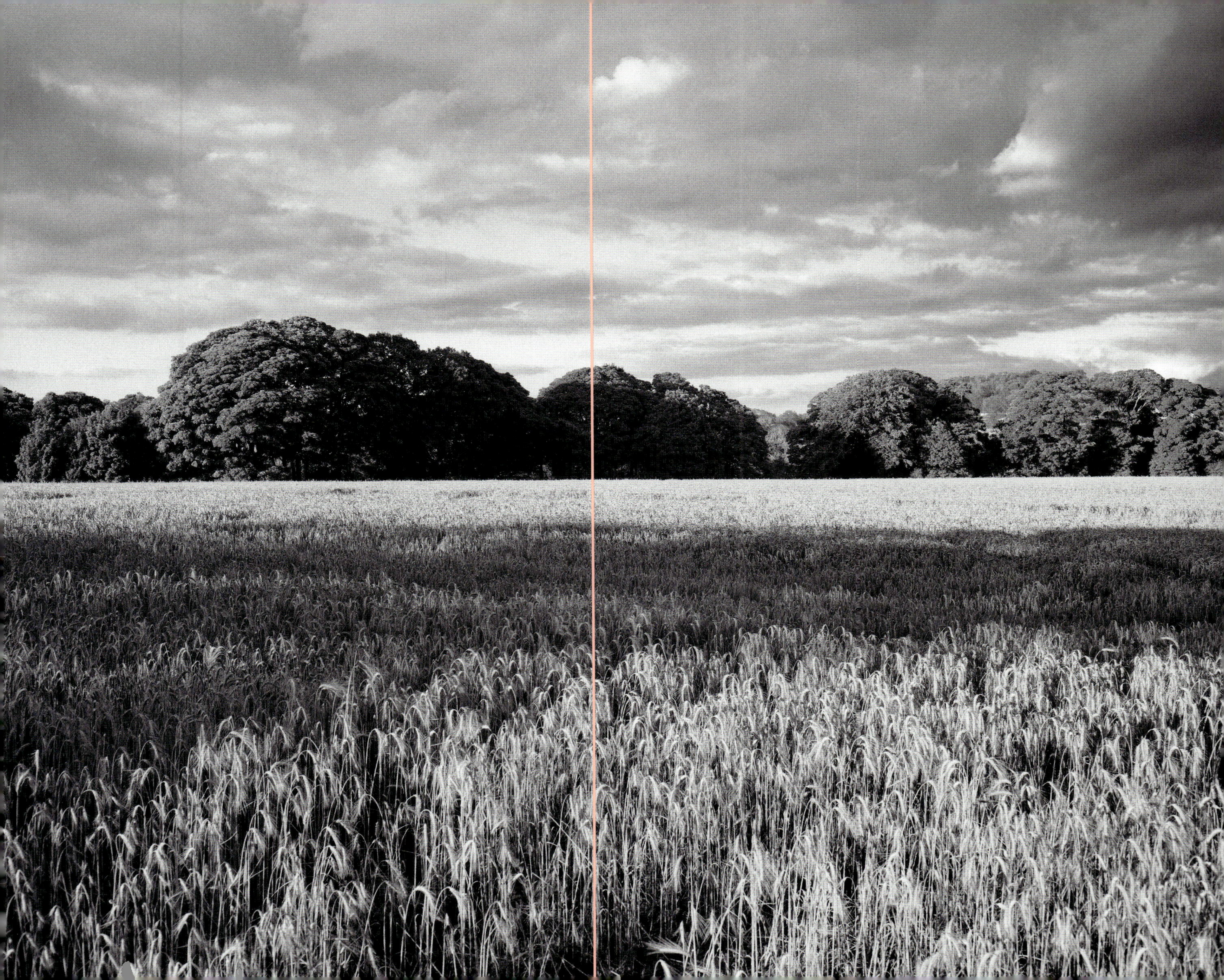

08.

00° 00′ 00″ longitude: River Welland tributary, near Holbeach St. Marks, Lincolnshire: △ N

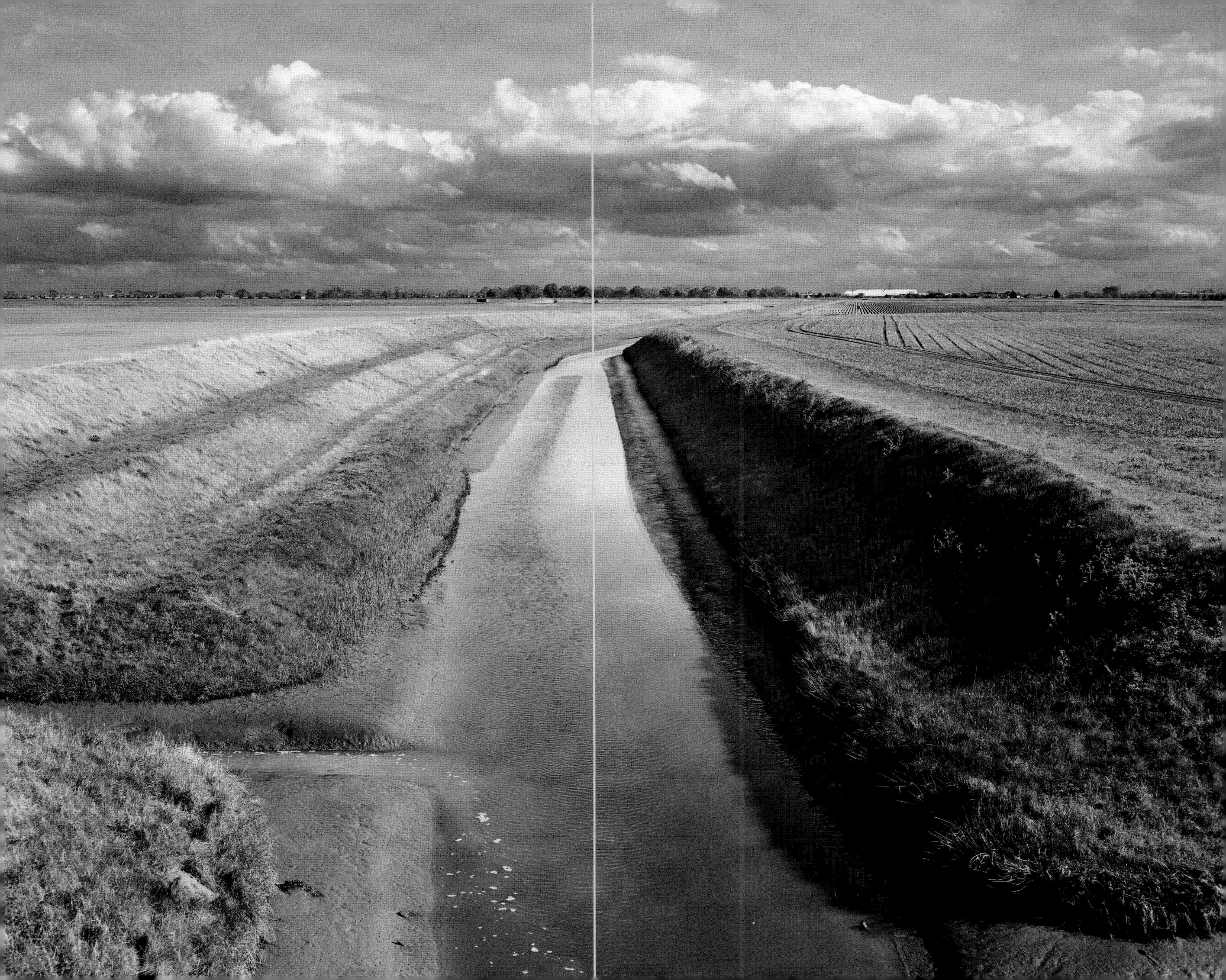

09.

00°00'00" longitude: Great Eversden, Cambridgeshire: ⌂N

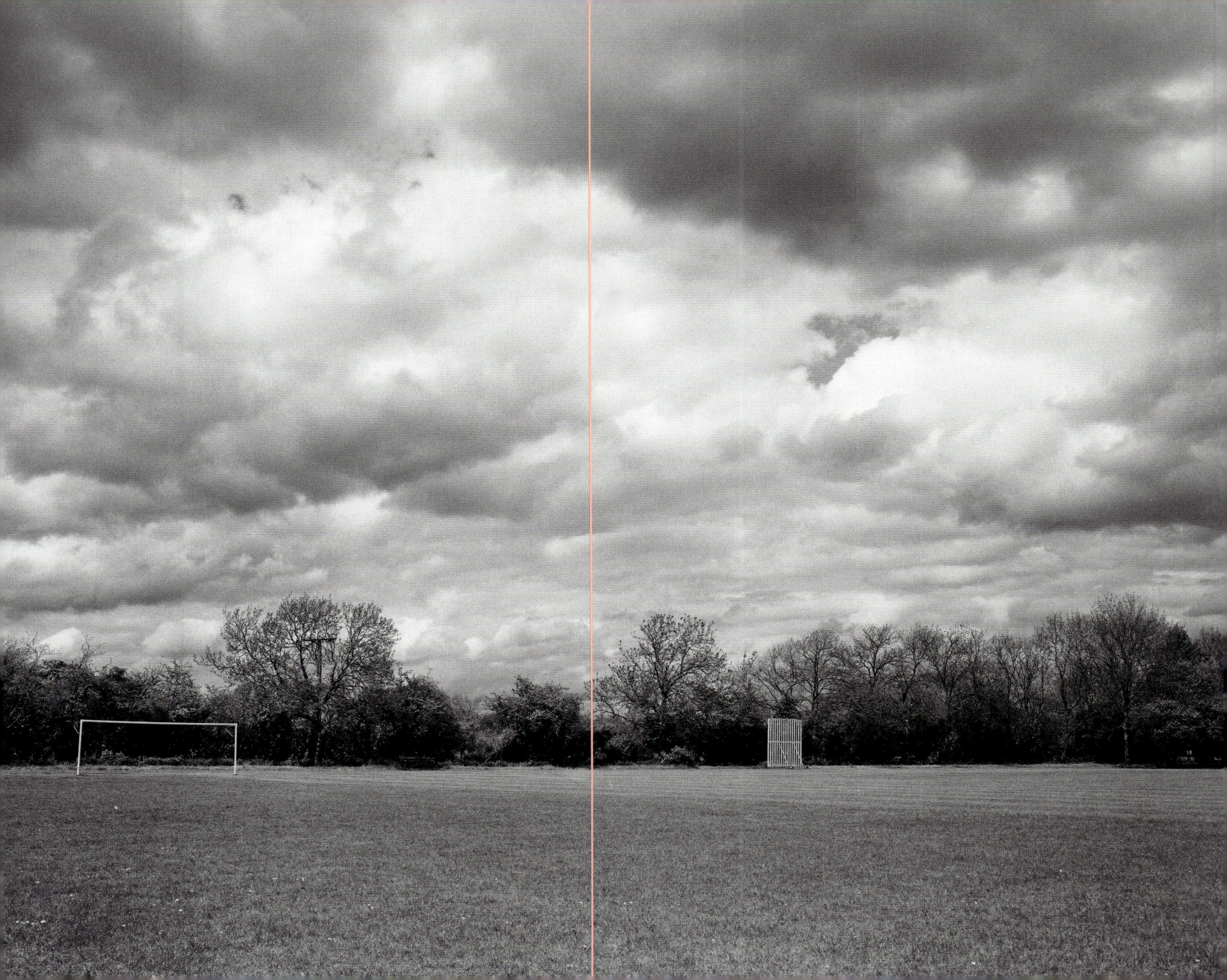

10.

00°00'00" longitude: Old Hall Green, Hertfordshire: △ N

11.

00° 00' 00" longitude: Lee Valley County Park, Essex: △N

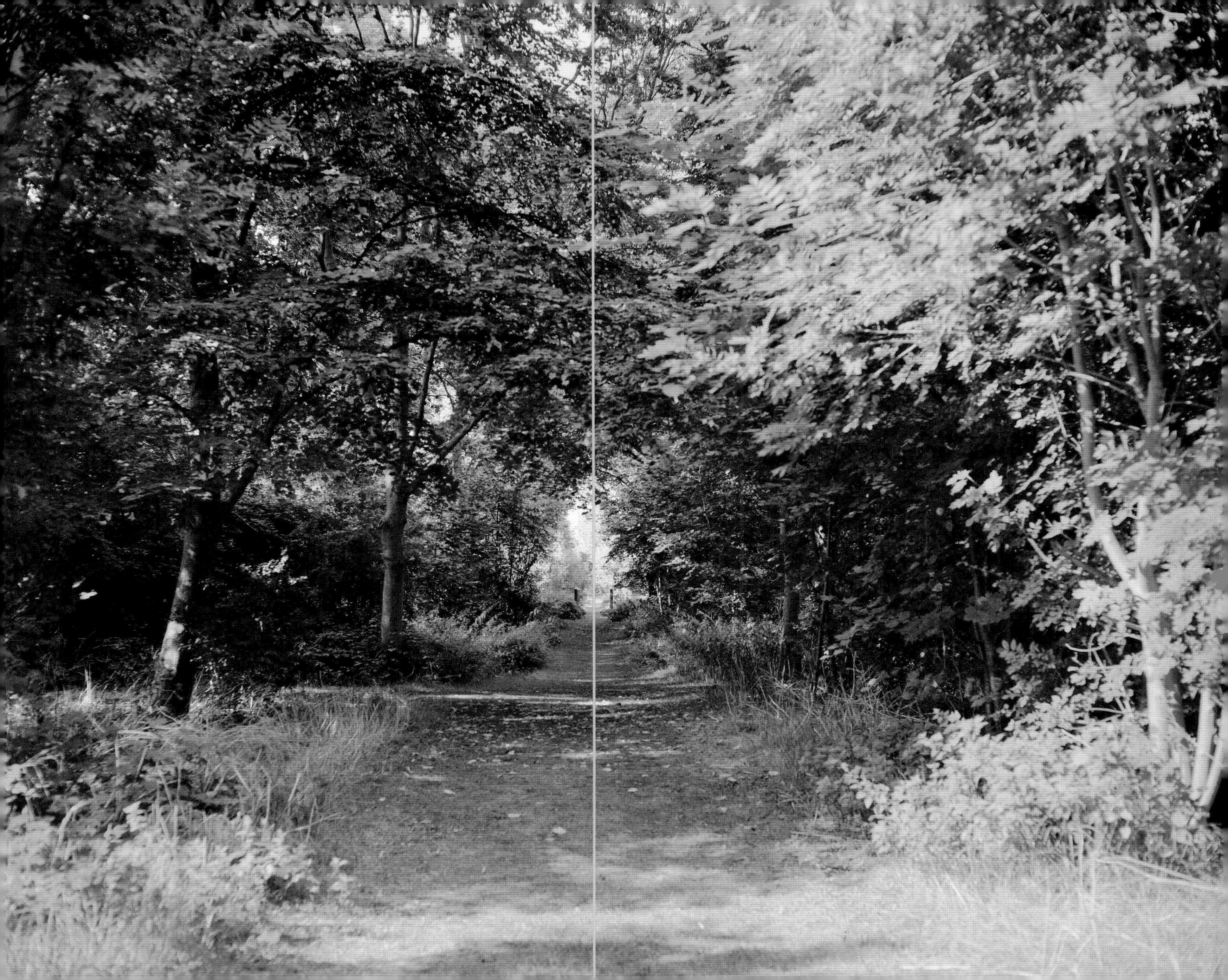

12.

00° 00′00″ longitude: Waltham Abbey Church, Essex: ▽S

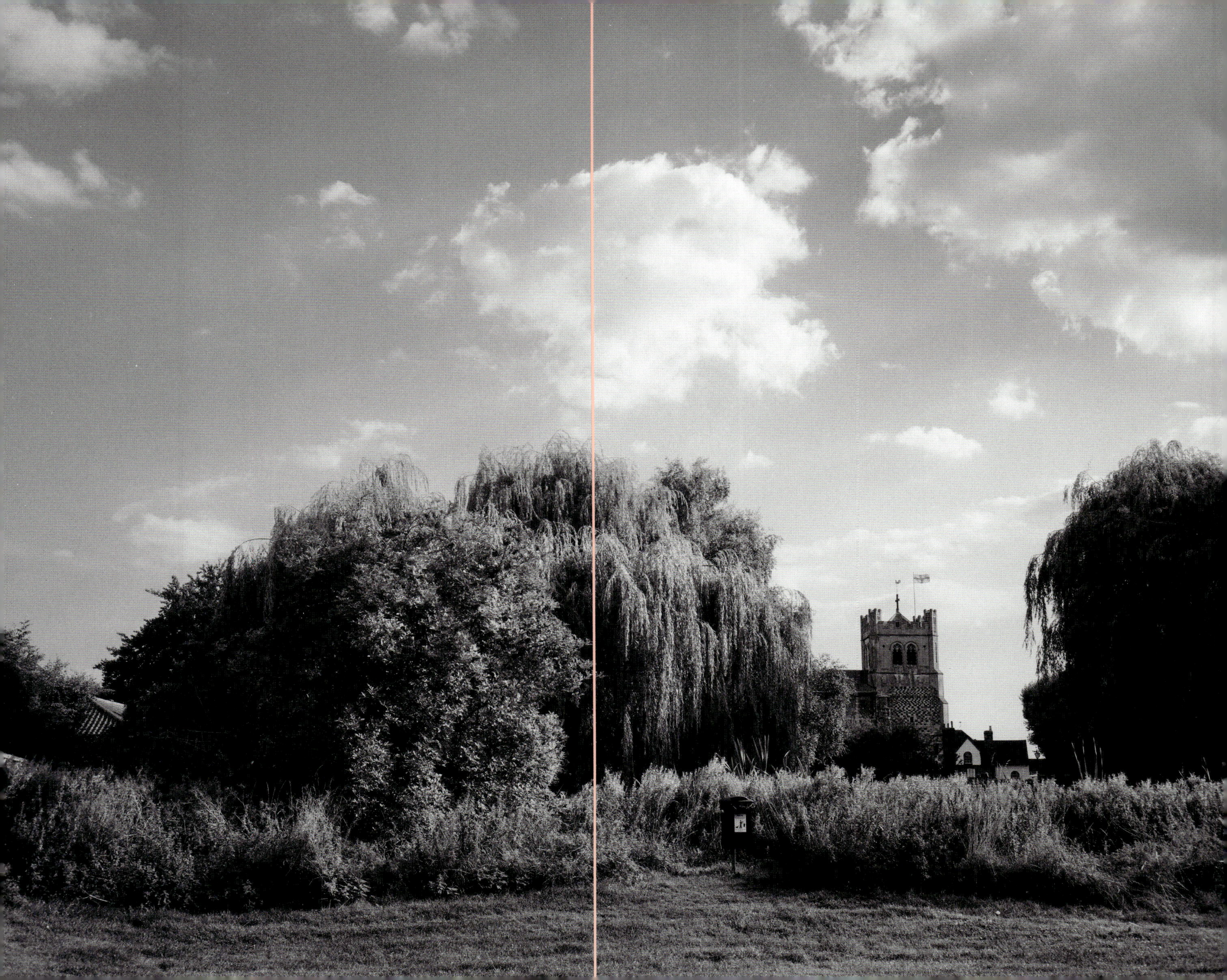

00° 00′ 00″ longitude: River Thames north of Greenwich, London: ◻ N

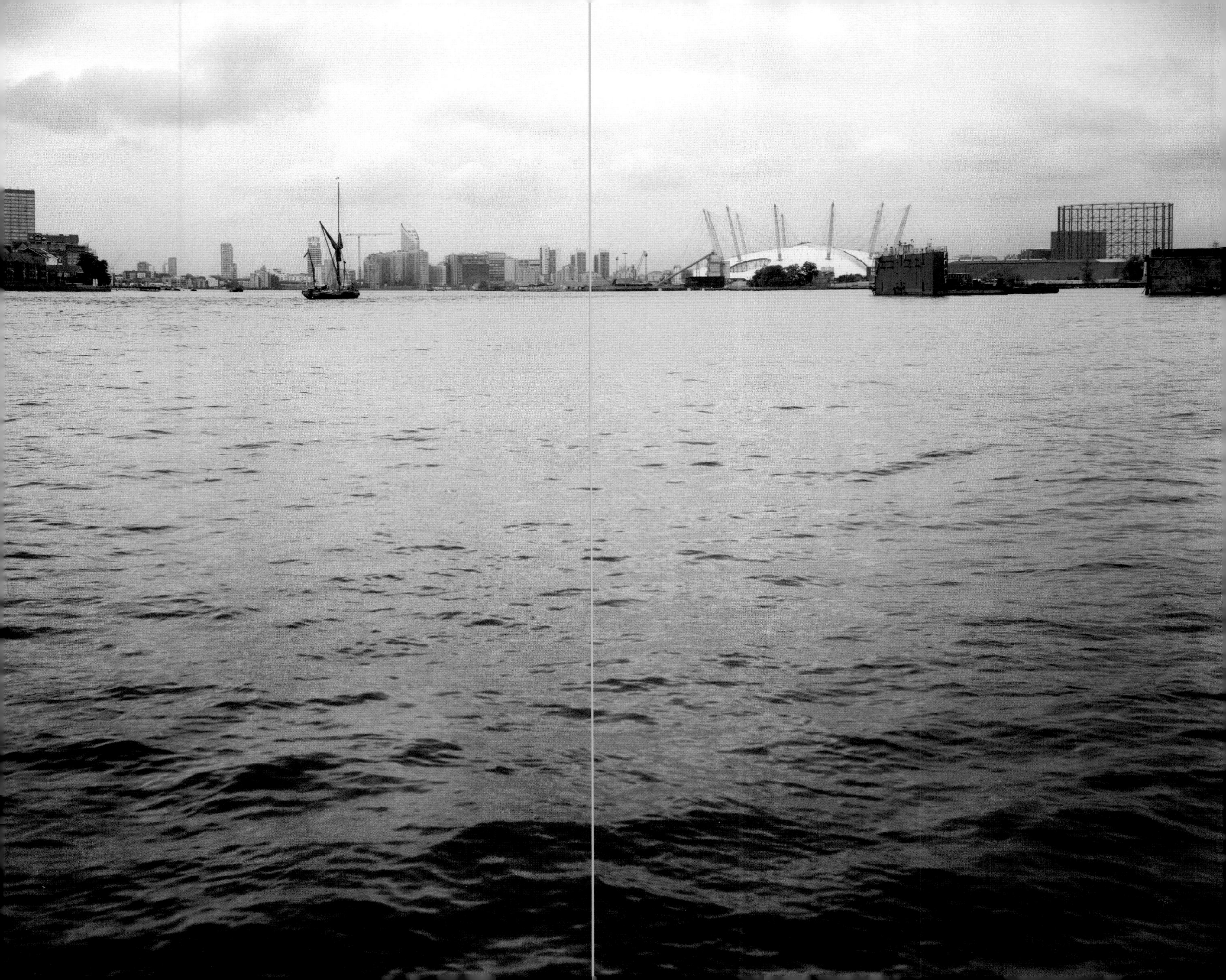

14.

00° 00′ 00″ longitude: Biggin Hill, Kent: ▽S

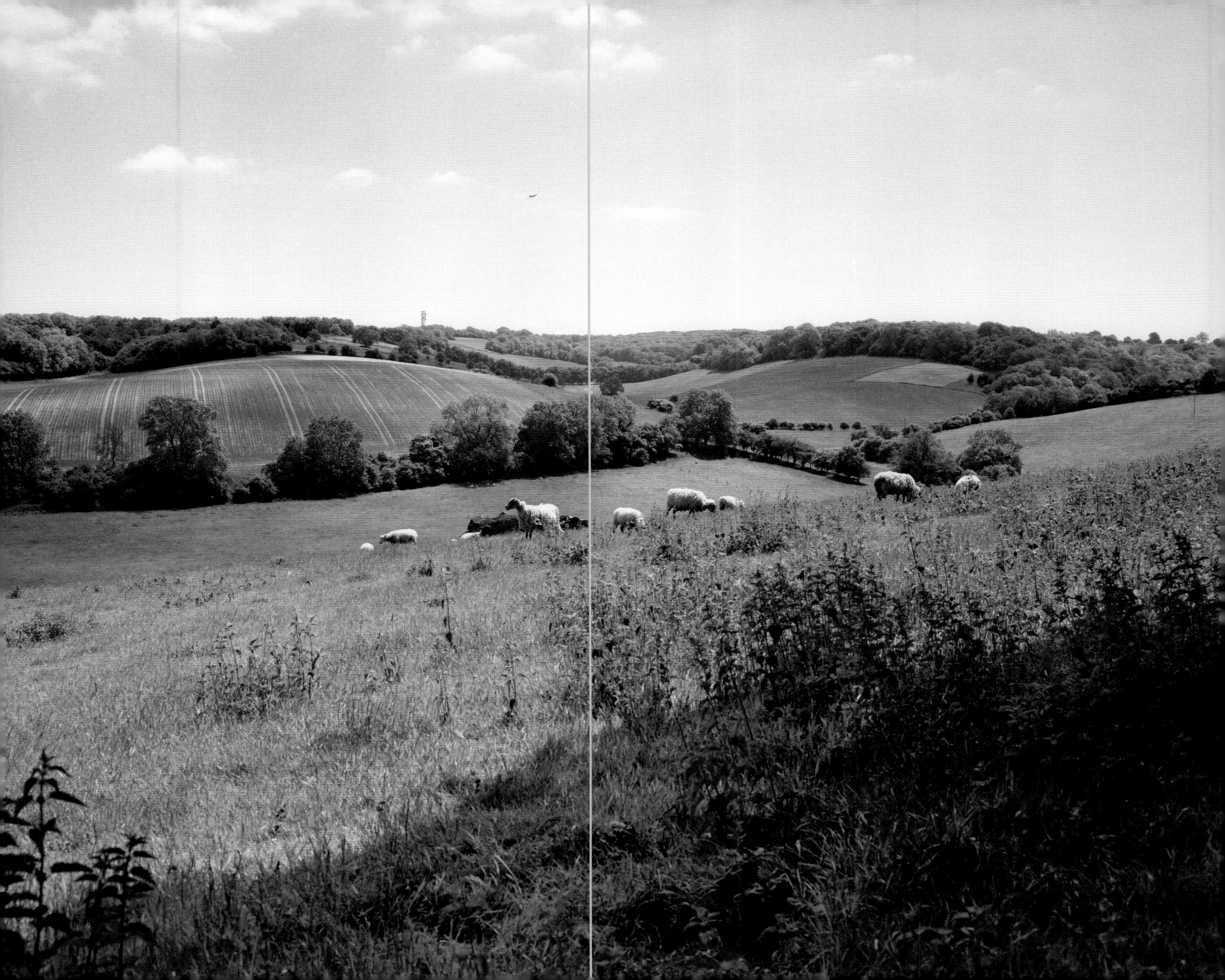

15.

00° 00' 00" longitude: Hamsey railway crossing, near Lewes, East Sussex: ▽S

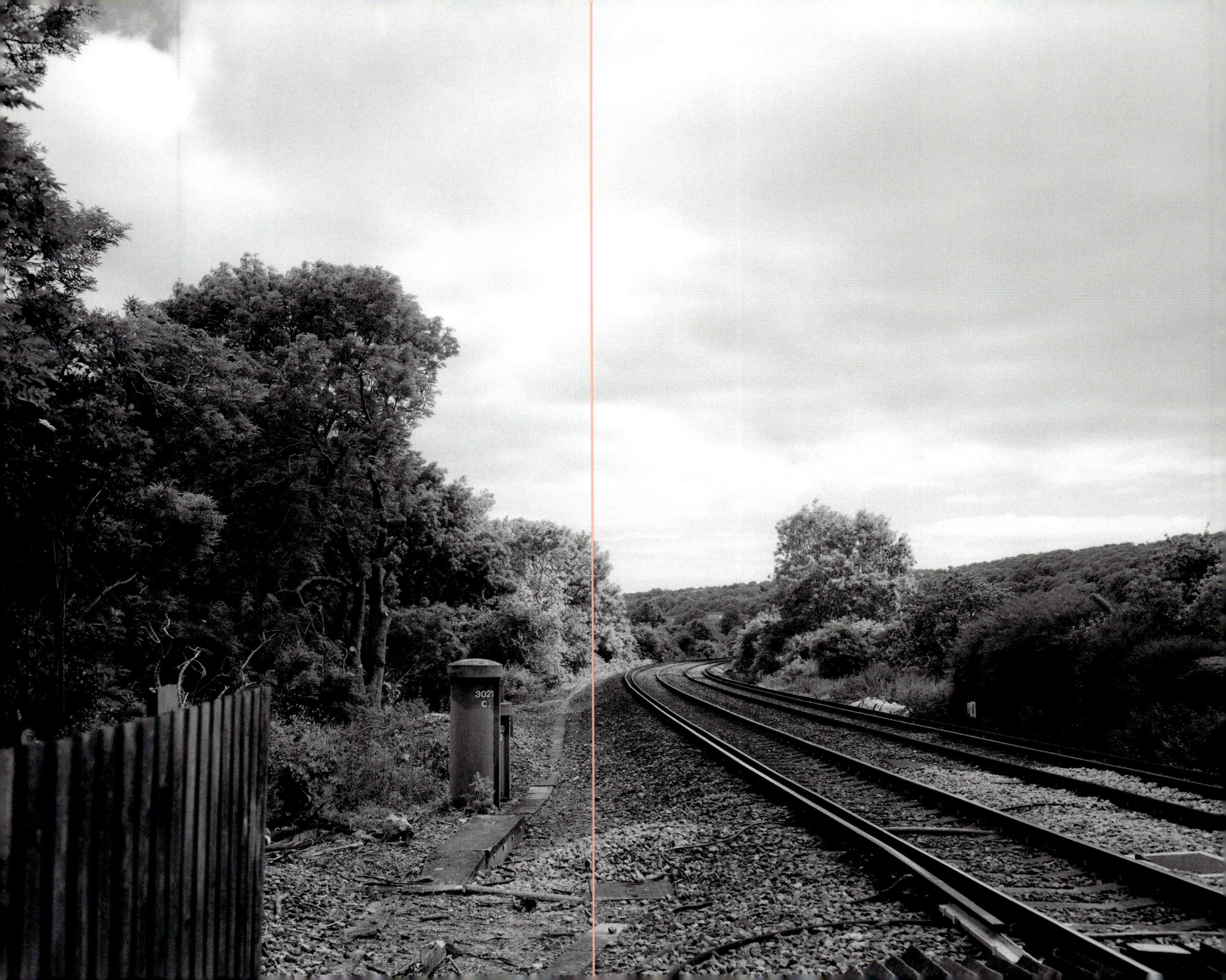

00°00′00″ longitude: English Channel, Peacehaven, East Sussex: ▽ S